Amazing People

KATHLEEN WILLS

Editorial Board
David Booth • Joan Green • Jack Booth

STECK-VAUGHN
⌐ Harcourt Achieve

www.HarcourtAchieve.com

10801 N. Mopac Expressway
Building # 3
Austin, TX 78759
1.800.531.5015

Steck-Vaughn is a trademark of Harcourt Achieve Inc. registered in the
United States of America and/or other jurisdictions. All inquiries should
be mailed to Harcourt Achieve Inc., P.O. Box 27010, Austin, TX 78755.

Ru'bĭcon © 2006 Rubicon Publishing Inc.
www.rubiconpublishing.com

Project Editors: Miriam Bardswich, Kim Koh
Editorial Assistant: Erin Doupe
Art/Creative Director: Jennifer Drew-Tremblay
Designer: Sarah Anderson

6 7 8 9 10   5 4 3 2 1

Amazing People
ISBN 1-41902-447-7

CONTENTS

We never know how high we are
Till we are called to rise;
And then, if we are true to plan,
Our statures touch the skies.

— EMILY DICKINSON

VICTIMS' CHAMPION
IS KILLED IN IRAQ

Marla Ruzicka leads a demonstration calling for U.S. compensation to victims of the recent U.S.-led military campaign in Afghanistan, April 7, 2002, outside of the U.S. Embassy in Kabul, Afghanistan.

warm up

With a partner, discuss the ways in which civilian victims of war differ from the soldiers who die fighting wars.

By Ellen Knickmeyer
Washington Post Foreign Service
Monday, April 18, 2005

"It's rare anybody in a lifetime can accomplish what she did, and she did it in just a couple years."

BAGHDAD, April 17 — In a one-woman battle for the victims of war, 28-year-old Marla Ruzicka won over Congress and the U.S. military, persuading the United States to free a precedent-setting $20 million for civilians it injured by mistake in Afghanistan and Iraq.

Ruzicka was killed Saturday on Baghdad's most dangerous road when a suicide bomber aiming for a U.S. convoy pulled up alongside her and detonated his explosives.

CHECKPOINT
Notice the tragic irony of Marla Ruzicka's death.

The blast also killed Ruzicka's longtime Iraqi aide and driver, Faiz Ali Salim, 43, as they drove the road to a U.S. military base by the airport, where foreigners travel for flights out of the country and where Iraqis go to ask for help from the American forces.

A security guard for the convoy was also killed. His identity had not been released by authorities.

"The ride is not pleasant. Military convoys passing every moment. Faiz and I hold our breath," Ruzicka wrote on June 25, 2004, in her online journal. "Such convoys in that area are the target of rockets and fire from the resistance. It would be nice if there was a more secure location for Iraqis to seek compensation."

"What she wanted to do was eminently sensible," Sen. Patrick J. Leahy (D-Vt.), who pushed through the compensation package after Ruzicka proposed it, said by telephone from the United States. "Unfortunately, things that are eminently sensible sometimes get lost in bureaucracy without a champion. She was a champion I would follow anywhere."

CHECKPOINT
How do these words give Marla's life's work credibility?

Two years ago, she founded a Washington-based organization called Campaign for Innocent Victims in Conflict.

"It's rare anybody in a lifetime can accomplish what she did, and she did it in just a couple years," Leahy said.

Ruzicka came from the isolated, hilly town of Lakeport, Calif. What started out as anti-war fervor during college took her to Washington, then to Afghanistan and Iraq.

"The amazing thing is she came here as an anti-war activist, really," said Tim Rieser, an aide to Leahy who worked closely with Ruzicka on compensating Afghan and Iraq families. But she "quickly saw that wasn't the way to accomplish what she felt strongest about, which was to help innocent people who

---

precedent: *previous case taken as an example for later cases*
convoy: *a group of vehicles traveling together*

eminently: *very*
bureaucracy: *officials and administrators in a government, often regarded as inflexible and controlling*
fervor: *passion*

A wounded Iraqi boy looks on following a bomb explosion Monday, October 25, 2004 near a U.S.- Australian military convoy in central Baghdad, Iraq.

were wounded — to get Congress, get the U.S. military to do that."

"In that sense, she accomplished what frankly nobody has ever accomplished," Rieser said. "Programs were created for Afghanistan and for Iraq to provide assistance to victims of U.S. military mistakes."

Ruzicka could get Bianca Jagger to a party in Kabul, win millions in public and private funds for war victims, and change the way the United States handled war, colleagues said.

Blonde, with hair variously in dreadlocks or extensions, Ruzicka could "talk, smile, and bust her way into all the meetings she needed — with Afghans, Iraqis, U.S. military, and U.S. Embassy people," said Quil Lawrence, a journalist who had met her in Kabul.

In Iraq, Ruzicka donned a neck-to-ankle black abaya, hiding her status as a foreigner to guard against being kidnapped, and met with families of Iraqis who had been killed in the war. Salim, a pilot with Iraqi Airways, was won over enough to drive her for two years and to keep her project going when Iraq became too dangerous for her to work.

On the day of the U.S. handover of sovereignty to Iraq, Salim wrote of a typical scene for Ruzicka in Baghdad: dealing with danger with black robes flapping. "The day of the handover Marla and I were annoyed because they would not let us over the July 14th Bridge that connects Baghdad with the Green Zone. So I dropped Marla off in her abaya and watched her jump over the concrete blocks to cross the bridge on foot. I knew she would find a ride. So two minutes later I called her and she was in a car.

CHECKPOINT
What does this tell you about Marla's personality?

sovereignty: *independence; having power or authority*

"Ruzicka could get Bianca Jagger to a party in Kabul, win millions in public and private funds for war victims and change the way the United States handled war"...

Salim's friends begged him for two years to stop working with Americans, saying it was too dangerous, one colleague said Saturday, accompanying Salim's brother to track down his body. Salim is survived by his wife and a 2-month-old daughter.

CHECKPOINT

Notice how the next two paragraphs leave the reader with a feeling of foreboding.

This time Ruzicka stayed in Baghdad longer than she had planned because she believed she had found the key to establishing that the U.S. military kept records of its civilian victims, despite its official statements otherwise, colleagues said.

On Friday, a day before she died, two car bombs killed 18 people in the neighborhood where Ruzicka was staying with foreign journalists. The explosions also knocked out water to some in the neighborhood. Ruzicka led journalists to her hotel room — borrowed from another journalist — so they could shower.

On the way, she passed a wedding party gathering outside the hotel. "A sign of normal life!" Ruzicka said. She stopped and gave the women in the wedding party a kiss on each cheek. Apprehensive at the sign of Americans at first, the women were beaming in delight by the time she left.

Apprehensive: *fearful*

wrap up

1. As an Iraqi, what personal struggles do you think Faiz Ali Salim faced helping an American seek money for civilian victims of war?

2. Do you think Marla's story will inspire you to become more politically and socially active in your life? Why or why not? Discuss your responses with a partner.

3. Write an obituary of 100 to 150 words capturing Marla's personality as well as describing her accomplishments in her short 28 year lifespan.

WEB CONNECTIONS

1. Go to **www.civicworldwide.org** and click on the "About Us" link. Read through the postings and write a report explaining how the U.S. military determines their responsibility for Iraqi deaths.

2. Go to **www.civicworldwide.org** and click on the "View a slideshow of CIVIC's work in Iraq" link. View one of the slideshows and write a personal response to the images presented. Why do you think these images were chosen? What emotional reactions do you have to the photos?

Kenya James
Teen Entrepreneur
By Andrea Damewood

warm up

What magazines do you read? What kinds of articles do they have that you like? What topics would you like to see covered in teen magazines?

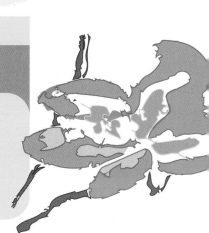

CHECKPOINT

Notice five things that Kenya James has done that most teens haven't.

What three features of *Blackgirl Magazine* make it different from other teen magazines?

James' accomplishments left many in the crowd stunned, regardless of her age. "I look at her and my mouth just hangs open …"

As founder, creative editor, and publisher of *Blackgirl Magazine*, Kenya James, like many executives, keeps a busy schedule. Between appearances on *Oprah* and *CNN*, and interviews with celebrities from OutKast to Lauryn Hill, she is currently developing her own clothing line and film company.

And she's still in high school.

James, 14, spoke during a April 5, [2004] Crain Lecture, "The Making of a Magazine," of the difficulties she has faced and the knowledge she has gained in starting her publication.

"I wanted a magazine for girls my age, my color and my culture," said James, who started *Blackgirl* two years ago. "As we continue to publish our issues, we move closer to being the voice of black girls."

The publication now boasts about 5,000 subscribers, James told the audience in the McCormick Tribune Center Forum, and will soon publish its ninth issue. *Blackgirl* features content written almost exclusively by teens, which makes it easy for readers to digest, she said.

Blackgirl departs from the average teen magazine by featuring true-to-life stories, as well as culture and history sections.

"We have a lynching survivor write about how he was spared," James said. "One of the key aspects of the magazine is history, because without history, we don't have a game plan for the future."

The magazine's cover page features ordinary girls instead of airbrushed supermodels.

CHECKPOINT
What are some difficulties that James faces in trying to publish a magazine?

The most challenging aspect of publishing the magazine, James said, is not managing her time but finding advertisers to generate revenue. She is attempting to solve this problem by networking through the Atlanta Association of Black Journalists and other local media outlets.

Obtaining interviews with pop culture icons hasn't been easy either.

"They were shocked that an 11- or 12-year-old girl was calling them," James said. "I got the runaround with the record companies but finally I was able to get an interview with OutKast."

James strives to maintain professionalism during interviews, but her excitement for interviewing rapper Bow Wow showed that she's also still a teenager.

"When I was talking to him on the phone, it was straight business," she said. "But when I got off the phone, it was on!"

James, an only child, said she got her interest in publishing from her mother, Karen, who quit her job as head of marketing at Elektra Records to start her own business. James said her mother's philosophy that "children should not have free time" has taught her to stay organized while maintaining a healthy balance between work and personal time.

"Children will rise to the expectations we set … if you plant the seeds early, they will grow," her mother said. "I think if Kenya weren't doing the magazine, she'd be doing something equally significant."

James' accomplishments left many in the crowd stunned, regardless of her age. "I look at her and my mouth just hangs open," said Selisa Simmons-Frazier, 25, editor and publisher of a national newsletter for black women called "SistahSpeak!"

"I think back to when I was her age, and it never would have occurred to me to start a magazine. Most adults would be hesitant to do the things she's done."

wrap up

1. With a partner, brainstorm ideas for a teen magazine. What type of magazine would you create to reflect your interests? What name would you give it? What kinds of articles would you put in your magazine? Who would you get to advertise in your magazine?

2. Create a list of people that you would like to interview for your magazine. Explain why you would like to interview them.

SKYWALKERS

By Richard Hill

Sky image—istockphoto; CN Tower Worker—CSTM CN000706)

warm up

Have you been up to the viewing decks on any tall buildings? What did you see? How did you feel?

FYI

Ironworkers from Six Nations have not only worked throughout the U.S. and Canada, but also in other parts of the world, such as Russia and Africa.

They walk on steel beams towering in the sky, fearless of the distance between the skyscraper skeleton supporting them and the microscopic city below. Maintaining balance on a narrow beam over 1,200 feet in the sky would be impossible for most people, but not for thousands of American Indian Ironworkers who have built, and continue to build, impressive, gravity-defying skyscrapers around the world.

The history of American Indian Ironworkers dates back to 1850 when the Mohawk of Kahnawake (Caughnawaga) on the outskirts of Montreal earned a living as quarries for Canada's emerging construction boom. Rail lines had come to Kahnawake and the Mohawk men would ferry passengers back and forth to Montreal. When the Victoria railway bridge was being built, the Mohawks first supplied the stone for the large piers to support the steel bridge. The Mohawk laborers would wander out on the narrow beams and observe the work of the riveters.

quarries: *workers who move stone from where it was dug*
riveters: *workers who join pieces of metal together*

CHECKPOINT

Why do you think this section is set off in italics?

Tom Diabo, whose grandfather worked on that Victoria Bridge, remembers:

"You know how Mohawks love to build things. So when the men from town were watching the bridge being built, some of the younger guys just climbed right up to take a closer look at how it was being done. The French-men they had working there was so scared that they had to hold onto everything they could so they wouldn't fall off. Of course, the guys from town wasn't scared. They just walked along the supports looking the job over, and checking out how the job was done … This is how we got into the construction trade."

Traveling to cities like New York, Detroit, Buffalo, or wherever, was not an obstacle to the American Indian Ironworker. It was part of their lifestyle, of their tradition, and took the Ironworker to every state and province in North America. Unfortunately, death followed close behind. Paul Diabo, the first American Indian to work the iron in New York, also became the first to die in that city, as he fell from the Hell Gate Bridge and drowned in the river below.

American Indians have helped change the North American landscape, as they have worked on practically all the tallest buildings in the United States, Canada, and around the world. As Al Smith, an Ironworker from Six Nations who worked on the Verrazano- Narrows Bridge in New York puts it, "Almost all of New York above the 20-storey level has been built by Mohawks."

The image of the Ironworker as Mohawk, and the Ironworker in Manhattan, have become inseparable. Newspapers across North America continue to promote the legend of the fearless American Indian Ironworker:

"Virtually all of New York City's skyline has been built by American Indians. Mohawks are famed for their catlike agility, tightrope walker's balance, and indifference to heights." (*Parade*, January 31, 1982)

CHECKPOINT

Notice the characteristics that make Mohawks good skywalkers.

In fact, American Indian Ironworkers helped construct New York City's famous twin towers. Following the terrorist attacks, American Indian Ironworkers assisted in safely dismantling what remained of the towers.

Darryl Pronovost, a 38-year-old Mohawk from Kahnawake, near Montreal, helped with the cleanup operation of the twin towers after 9/11. At the end of one shift in September, he created a model of the twin towers out of steel from the rubble by shaping it with a blowtorch. Pronovost used his blowtorch to mould steel crosses and twin-tower models for victims' families, firefighters, and elected officials. "I wanted to make something so people could take something home with them, because it's a shame — they're going to melt all the steel down."

(*TORONTO STAR*, January 19, 2002)

wrap up

Imagine you are a reporter on a construction site with the Skywalkers. Write a report about these "fearless Ironworkers" for your newspaper. Be certain to give it a catchy headline.

Reflections: Tribute to Our Skywalkers, 1983. The Artist: Arnold Jacobs

THE CALL OF THE RESERVE

By Brant Maracle, an Ironworker turned poet

"Hear the call of the Reserve, (Territory)
    your home,
You mighty men of the Mohawks.
Come down from your lofty heights,
And leave the steel for another day,
It is time to wend your way.
The beating of the drum does call,
Beneath it your heart will surely fall.

From Caughnawaga, St. Regis, Six Nations
    and Tyendinaga too,
Come the mighty Mohawks,
Who have unflinchingly borne the steel,
    A task done well,
Certainly a story it does tell.

Your class and inherent knowledge you
    have lent,
As beneath your hands the steel hath bent.
Pliers, rivets, coil these tools alone your
    trade,
as money, and history you have surely
    made. ...

But, above the noise of the streets,
The heart of the Mohawk does beat,
For the Reserve where the last bastion,
Of Mohawk culture doth meet.

So cometh weeks long end,
The heart of the Mohawk does wend,
For home and family and friends.

The sweet grass with its fragrant smell,
The blackash with its aroma well,
The Longhouse with its message tell,
The Gustoah you shall wear well,

Trees and splendid canoe,
Lacrosse, bow and arrow, shotgun too,
Gusty winds and rising waves,
Calls the heart of the Indian brave,
Come back my Love.

Wend your way home, oh Mohawk,
For home is where your people dwell,
There you shall find a tale to tell,
Find the culture and customs of your
    people intact,
And wear your beauty back."

---

wend: *make one's way*
bastion: *center of support*
Gustoah: *a type of Iroquois headdress*

wrap up

1. What customs call the Mohawks back to the reserve?

2. The poem tells the story of the Mohawk Ironworkers. Write the main idea of each stanza in one sentence to create a summary of the poem.

3. Which account of the Skywalkers — the article or the poem — do you prefer? Explain why in a short paragraph.

15

warm up

What would cause a democratic government to confine someone to his or her home?

How can one small woman pose a threat to an entire government? In democratic countries, people vote for the person they want to lead their country. But in Burma (now known as Myanmar), where a junta rules the country, nobody gets to vote.

Aung San Suu Kyi thinks that isn't the best way to rule Burma and has been trying since 1988 to bring democracy to Burma.

CHECKPOINT
Notice how Suu Kyi's family has inspired her.

Suu Kyi's family has played an important role in Burma's history. Her father helped bring about his country's independence and was assassinated when Suu Kyi was only two years old. Later, her mother was the Burmese ambassador for India.

Although she left Burma to go to school in India and later England, where she married and had two children, Suu Kyi remained close to Burma. In 1988, when her mother was sick, Suu Kyi returned to Burma alone.

At that time it seemed like Burma might become democratic. With her family history Suu Kyi ran for government as the leader of the National League for Democracy (NLD) and won. The corrupt military government refused to recognize this and put the pro-democracy leaders, including Suu Kyi, under house arrest.

Despite the restrictions of house arrest, Suu Kyi continued to campaign for democracy and for her efforts and sacrifices won the Nobel Peace Prize in 1991. She was unable to accept the prize in person and her two sons and her husband, with a picture of Suu Kyi facing the audience, accepted the prize. In his speech presenting the prize to her sons, Professor Francis Sejersted, chairman of the Nobel committee, declared, "Her absence fills us with fear and anxiety. We ordinary people, I believe, feel that with her courage and her high ideals, Aung San Suu Kyi brings out something of the best in us."

junta: *a political or military group taking power after a revolt*

A Myanmar (Burmese) activist demands the release of Aung San Suu Kyi outside the Myanmar Embassy in Thailand, June 9, 2003.

FYI

Suu Kyi's imprisonment caused an international outcry. World leaders called for her release and democratic countries are applying economic and political pressures.

Suu Kyi's political party, the National League for Democracy, won 80% of the seats in parliament in the 1990 election — a popular verdict the military regime still refuses to accept.

they would not guarantee that she would be allowed to return. She chose her country over her family. Her husband died without being able to say goodbye to Suu Kyi.

In 2000, then U.S. President Bill Clinton, upon awarding her The Presidential Medal of Freedom noted, "She sits confined … in her home in Rangoon, unable to speak to her people or the world. Her struggle continues and her spirit still inspires us. She has seen her supporters beaten, tortured, and killed, yet she has never responded to hatred and violence in kind. All she has ever asked for is peaceful dialogue. The only weapons the Burmese people have are the words of reason and the example of this astonishingly brave woman."

Suu Kyi remained under house arrest until 1995 when she was "freed." "Free" has an entirely different meaning for Suu Kyi. She has, since 1988, spent eight of her last 15 birthdays behind bars, been put in jail, or held under house arrest for such crimes as campaigning for the National League for Democracy.

In 1999, with her family back in England, not even the news that her husband was deathly ill made her abandon her goal of bringing democracy to Burma. While the government agreed to let Suu Kyi go to England for one last visit with her husband,

CHECKPOINT

How do the quotation marks change the meaning of the word "free"?

wrap up

1. In your own words, explain why Suu Kyi was placed under house arrest.

2. Read the second last paragraph. Write a letter from Suu Kyi to her husband explaining why she cannot visit him one last time before he dies.

meet the napster

BY KARL TARO GREENFELD

warm up

What personality traits do you think set inventors apart from the rest of us?

TIME, OCTOBER 2, 2000

CHECKPOINT

As you read this article, notice how Shawn Fanning is described.

At dawn, Shawn Fanning lay on the brown carpet in the shadow of a converted bar counter, consumed by the idea. He had been awake 60 straight hours writing code on his notebook computer. His idea was big and frightening and full of implications, and it filled him up. This 18-year-old college dropout was sprawled on the floor in his uncle's office, across the street from the breaking waves in Hull, Massachusetts.

Fanning only dimly recalls that period in mid-1999, when he wrote the source code for the music file-sharing program called Napster. He can't remember specific months, weeks, or days. He was just hunched over his Dell notebook, writing the software and crashing on his uncle's sofa or the floor. Then he'd shake off fatigue, scarf a bowl of cereal and sit back down. He worked feverishly because he was sure someone else had the same idea, that any day now some software company or media conglomerate would be unveiling a version of the same application, and then Fanning's big idea wouldn't be his anymore.

And he believed in it because his idea was so simple: a program that would allow computer users to swap music files with one another directly, without going through a centralized file server or middle man. All he had to do was combine the features of existing programs: the instant-messaging system of Internet Relay Chat, the file-sharing functions of Microsoft Windows, and the advanced searching and filtering capabilities of various search engines.

For its users, Napster has become another appliance, like a toaster or washing machine. Call it the music appliance: log on, download, play songs. The simplicity of the program is part of its genius. Since he took only three months to write the source code, Fanning says he didn't have time to make it more complicated. "I had to focus on functionality, to keep it real simple," he says in his gravelly monotone. "With a few more months, I might have added a lot of stuff that would have screwed it up. But in the end, I just wanted to get the thing out." …

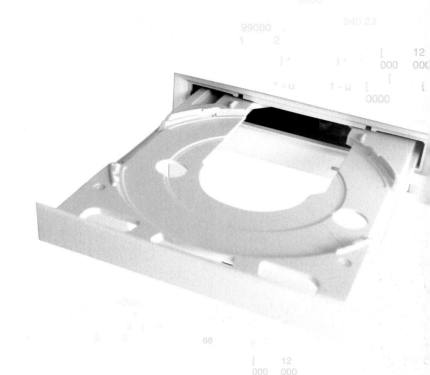

CHECKPOINT

Identify the simile and metaphor used at the beginning of the paragraph to show how Napster is an important part of everyday life.

---

conglomerate: *a group of companies that have joined together*
functionality: *practicality*

Shawn Fanning plays a guitar with Sean Parker, his co-founder of Napster.com. ▶

Fanning never intended to hijack the music industry. The idea for Napster just came to him as he was sitting in his dorm room at Northeastern University in Boston, hanging out with his bros … and listening to his roommate whine about dead MP3 links. Fanning, whose high school nickname was the Napster (a reference to his perpetually nappy hair), just shrugged. But he began thinking there might be a way to access files without going through a website.

One January evening, while riding back to campus with his cousin Brian Fanning, Shawn got out of the car and began walking up the path. After two steps, he stopped. "I'm not going back to school," he told his cousin. Brian shrugged and drove off. It was Shawn's problem.

"When he didn't go back to school, it crushed me," recalls Coleen Verrier, Fanning's mom. "But he explained he had these things he said were urgent." Fanning was unfazed. He felt he had no choice. He never went back to his dorm room, leaving behind his clothes, books and bedding. He took his computer with him, of course.

As the creator of Napster, Fanning has reached a level of fame unprecedented for a 19-year-old who is neither a sports hero nor a pop star. He's been on the cover of *Fortune, Business Week, Forbes,* and the *Industry Standard* and has been profiled just about everywhere else. Strangers pick him out at the mall buying a burrito or watching a San Francisco Giants game or just driving around in his newly customized Mazda RX-7.

nappy: *kinky*

"I don't think a day goes by when people don't recognize me." He introduced Britney Spears at the MTV Video Music Awards. Nike has offered him a shoe deal.

He lives *frugally*, as do more than a few billionaires in Silicon Valley, sharing a two-bedroom San Mateo apartment and a 72-inch wide-screen Mitsubishi television with co-Napsterite Sean Parker. The furniture is rented, the brown sofa often serving as a crash site for Fanning's 13-year-old brother, Raymond, who is teaching himself to code while he stays with Fanning. They have never bothered to get a phone line installed; the cellphone works just fine.

Shawn Fanning has become surprisingly thoughtful and well spoken — perhaps because, being at the center of an *epochal* lawsuit, he has had to. Meanwhile, there is another big idea he is dying to work out that could be bigger than Napster. What he is seeking to recapture are those days back in Hull, when it was just Fanning and Napster. When there were no lawsuits and no one to answer to and he was left alone to work on this little program of his, this idea that he would launch into the world. ...

frugally: *costing little*
epochal: *groundbreaking; setting a new direction*

wrap up

1. Shawn Fanning went from being a typical college kid to being the creator and part owner of Napster. With that has come a certain amount of fame and fortune. List examples of how Fanning's life has changed.

2. As a newspaper editor, reduce this article to 200-250 words.

"At that time I couldn't always see Jesse's face from my position behind the wheelchair. It wasn't until later when I saw pictures like this one that I realized how, at times, the journey was very tiring for Jesse."

JESSE'S JOURNEY

For 124 days, my son and I persevered through the blackflies, the rain, high winds, smoke from forest fires, and incredible heat.

By John Davidson

How far would you go for someone you love? That's a question that I asked myself after one of my sons was diagnosed with a disease for which there is no cure.

My wife Sherene and I are the parents of three boys, Tyler, Jesse, and Tim. At the age of five, Jesse was diagnosed with a disease called Duchenne Muscular Dystrophy (DMD). Almost 23,000 in North America have this disease that affects boys almost exclusively — and most do not live beyond their teen years.

Realizing that the fight against DMD lies in research, I set out to make a difference in the lives of all those boys, including my own son.

In May 1995, at the Manitoba-Ontario border, I began pushing Jesse in his wheelchair along the Trans-Canada Highway to raise money for research. The project quickly came to be known as "Jesse's Journey."

Duchenne Muscular Dystrophy: *general weakness and wasting of muscle*

warm up

- What is the most thoughtful thing someone ever did for you?

- With a partner, brainstorm incredible journeys that helped raise awareness about a social issue or disease.

In the rain, Jesse, Sherene, and I were escorted by the London Police color guard and pipe and drum band to a reception at Victoria Park.

CHECKPOINT

Notice the conditions John and Jesse had to endure and the response they received from supporters. It was the experience of a lifetime. But, would you do it?

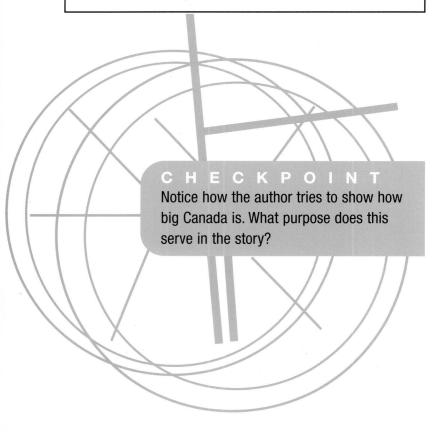

FYI

In 2003, *The Guinness Book of World Records* recognized John and Jesse Davidson's 286-day journey as a world record for the fastest crossing of Canada on foot.

What does it take to cross Canada? It took John Davidson six pairs of running shoes and lots of food — 635 loaves of bread, 41 jars of jam, 24 jars of peanut butter, 500 lb. of bananas, 1,200 apples and 1,200 oranges, 48 cans of fruit cocktail and, of course, 40 bags of nachos, among other items.

CHECKPOINT

Notice how the author tries to show how big Canada is. What purpose does this serve in the story?

For 124 days, my son and I persevered through the blackflies, the rain, high winds, smoke from forest fires, and incredible heat. Along the Trans-Canada Highway and the roads of Southern Ontario, we met thousands and thousands of supporters who cheered us on. Members of Parliament from every party stood and applauded as Jesse and I were recognized in the House of Commons in Canada's capital city, Ottawa. Tired and tanned from a summer on the road, we returned home to London, Ontario, after raising more than CDN $1.5 million for research.

Our story didn't end there.

Three years later, I was on the road again. Although it was an even bigger project this time, I was alone as Jesse's health would not permit him to come along. After dipping my shoes in the Atlantic Ocean just outside St. John's, Newfoundland, I set out to walk across Canada, the second largest country in the world and the largest country in the Western Hemisphere.

On January 20, 1999, I reached Beacon Hill Park in Victoria, British Columbia, 286 days after I began my quest to walk every step of the way across a vast country that spans six-and-a-half time zones.

In our travels, Jesse and I met and shook the hands of Canadians from every walk of life. After our journey across Ontario, we were asked to assist Her Majesty Queen Elizabeth II in planting a tree in London's Victoria Park to commemorate the wheelchair push across Ontario to raise money for research. Since we started our trek, we have been the center of a project that has raised more than CDN $7 million.

While building a fund that will generate money for research for years to come, Jesse and I also collected a huge treasure chest of memories along the way.

Along the Trans-Canada and the other highways that made up the route across Canada, people made donations from the windows of cars, vans, transport trucks, buses, and motor homes. Motorcyclists and people riding their bikes stopped to make donations. Others climbed down from farm and construction equipment. Even people on horseback wanted to take part in the magic of Jesse's Journey. Every day there were families waiting along city curbs or at the end of farm laneways to cheer on a determined father and son.

The Governor General of Canada presented us with the Meritorious Service Medal. Yet, for Jesse and me, the best memories are those from along the road. We will never forget the thousands of children who brought little jars of pennies, nickels, dimes, quarters, and loonies and toonies to the roadside.

The words "Jesse's Journey" still generate the image of a father pushing his son in a wheelchair along the Trans-Canada Highway in their quest to make life better for kids in Canada and around the world.

Painting by Ken Jackson

wrap up

1. Why do you think John Davidson's fundraising effort is called "Jesse's Journey"?

2. Identify five events John and Jesse have in their "treasure chest of memories."

3. Write a telephone conversation that John and one of his family members might have at the end of a long day of walking during his trek across Canada.

WEB CONNECTIONS

To learn more about Jesse's Journey and how you can become a part of the magic, visit **www.jessesjourney.com**.

LISA BENTLEY — *IRON WOMAN*

Lisa Bentley was already on her way to becoming a professional athlete when she was diagnosed with Cystic Fibrosis (CF) in her early 20s. A runner in university, Lisa swam and cycled to help her avoid injury. What started as a pastime turned into a passion. Determined not to let CF overshadow her goals, Lisa has been a six-time winner of Ironman competitions around the world and is still going strong. In 2004, BOLDPRINT interviewed this "Iron Woman."

warm up

What sports are you passionate about playing or watching?

BOLDPRINT: Were you always a dedicated competitor?

LISA BENTLEY: I took up running in grade five or six. I ran laps by myself around the school. I practiced in the morning before school started. In my first year of running, I came in 103rd in the cross-country meet. The next year, I came in fourth.

BP: What did you think you would be when you "grew up"?

LP: I've always wanted to be a teacher. I became a high-school Math and Computer teacher in 1992 and taught for seven years.

BP: Do you have memories of watching the Olympics and thinking you would one day like to compete in them?

LB: I remember watching the Olympics in 1984 when Joan Benoit won the marathon. She was a nobody and all of a sudden, this sprite of a woman is winning the Olympics. Fantastic!

Yes, I wanted to and still want to be an Olympian — I always wanted to be the "best" in my sport. Those Olympic dreams are fine as a child. As an adult, however, I realize that there is more to the Olympics than just being your best. You have to agree with the politics

CHECKPOINT

Notice the use of dashes in this answer. What effect do they create?

of the sport. You have to change with the sport as it changes to fit the Olympic mold. In many cases, you have to invest a lot of money to follow that dream. That was why I chose long-distance triathlon — it played to my strength as an ultra endurance athlete and I could survive financially by doing it.

BP: What is your fondest memory of competition at the elite level?

LB: Winning my first Ironman in New Zealand was an incredible memory. I had traveled away from home to train in Australia for six weeks prior to the race. It was very difficult for me to leave my family and my dogs. I remember crying for most of the 24-hour flight and then crying for most of the week once in New Zealand. It was a struggle. But it marked considerable growth for me as a person and as an athlete.

BP: You are a celebrity. Does being treated differently impress you?

LB: Being treated differently puts pressure on me. I am a normal person with fears and joys and highs and lows — I will win some races, but not all races.

BP: What do you consider to be the most challenging aspect of being a professional athlete?

LB: The training is very difficult. When I am in an Ironman building block (two months long) — I barely have the energy to speak to my coach to give him a training report; you are pushing your body daily for between three and eight hours per day. But it is also draining mentally because it is hard to focus on maintaining that high energy output all day long.

BP: Can you tell us what is going through your mind while you are racing?

LB: I continually feed my brain positive thoughts and images. I see myself being successful. I see myself doing all parts of my sport — swim, bike, and run — perfectly. I think about my nutrition — is it time to eat, drink, take a salt pill? I think about being good to myself — not beating myself or evaluating my performance (that comes later) — reminding myself that I am doing my best — asking myself if I can go harder — if I could be doing anything better. I think about my best races. I relive them.

BP: What role do you think your family, coach, and physiotherapist play in your success?

LB: My coach is central to the whole thing. Obviously, he takes care of my physical training but then there is also the mental training — I'd say that this is the part which makes me a champion. He has taught me how to "think" when I am racing — how to turn a negative into a positive — how to race internally (focus on self) rather than externally (worrying about others). He is a brilliant coach.

My physiotherapist is also crucial. I cannot compete if I am injured. He keeps my body healthy by having me do biomechanical work to strengthen my weak areas.

My family is also important — especially to the internal part of my racing. I race best when I am happy, and my family makes me happy.

CHECKPOINT

As you read Lisa's response to this question, notice the sacrifices that she has made to compete professionally. Would you be willing to make such a commitment?

BP: What sacrifices have you made to become a professional athlete?

LB: My life is completely scheduled. I am not free to do whatever. I need to rest on my days off as opposed to going out and doing something fun with friends. I have to watch my diet because it affects my performance. The day before a big workout, I would never go out to dinner and splurge on a decadent treat.

I train almost seven days per week — that is a huge commitment. When I finish a day at work, I am physically and mentally exhausted, which means that there isn't much energy left over for other people or other hobbies.

Holidays are on the back burner — I have six weeks of active recovery during my off season — that is when I have to schedule any holidays. Rarely could I go off to someone's cottage for a weekend in the summer because I am too busy training for a race.

BP: What do you do to relax?

LB: I walk my dogs — Brunswick and Madison — my black and brown labs. I love reading books that have to do with a person's inner spirit. My favorite books are *The Power of Positive Thinking,* by Norman Vincent Peale, and *The Power of One,* by Bryce Courtenay.

FYI

Ironman competitions include: swim 2.4 miles, bike 112 m, run 26.2 m. A tri-a-tri is less challenging — 410 yd. swim, 6 m bike, 1.5 m run.

BP: Do you think of retiring? If you weren't competing, what would you be doing?

LB: Yes, I think about retiring. Depending on where my life is at, I may stop competing at the end of the 2005 season. I would love to have a family, and as a woman, I would have to stop competing in order to make that happen. Now that I have built this career, I may pursue a career as a TV sports commentator, a professional coach, or a motivational speaker.

BP: Tell me one of your proudest moments.

LB: Meeting Tracey Richardson and her two kids — Cameron and Makena — the day after Ironman New Zealand. Her kids have CF and we had a good chat about it. After that meeting, Tracey decided to race an Ironman in order to raise money for CF.

Cystic Fibrosis in Lisa's Life:

CF affects sodium levels. When racing, Lisa has to drink enough water to process salt pills that she takes. Otherwise her muscles will cramp.

CF affects the immune system. Lisa has to eat well and avoid big crowds in order to stay healthy. Lisa suffers for a long time if she gets a chest infection.

Raising awareness of CF: Lisa is a role model for others, like New Zealander Tracey Richardson. The mother of two kids with CF, Tracey raised $82,000 by completing her first Ironman.

wrap up

1. In a small group, discuss all the things Lisa sacrifices to compete in her sport. Which do you think is the most difficult thing for her to go without? Why?

2. Of her coach, physiotherapist, and family, who do you think provides Lisa with the most support to compete in her sport? Why? Write a pre-race email or letter of encouragement from this person to Lisa.

Lisa Bently Photos-Kathleen Wills

WEB CONNECTIONS

Go to **www.xtri.com/athletes/lisabentley/** to find out more about Lisa's Ironman wins.

Aussies Swim

It is amazing how quickly things can go wrong. One minute you are enjoying a lovely afternoon of fishing and the next, you're clinging to the bottom of an upturned boat. In that split second when good goes bad, your life is changed forever.

warm up

Hindsight is 20/20. Looking back on an event that went wrong, can you recall what happened when things went bad? Knowing what you know now, what would you change in future?

THE SOUTHWESTERN TIP OF AUSTRALIA

Port Turton

WEDGE ISLAND

Pondalowie Bay

Stenhouse Bay

CHECKPOINT

How does the use of italics change the meaning of the word *safely*?

ON OCTOBER 1, 2000, 17-year-olds Ross Weaver and Trent Gardner and four friends were returning from a morning of fishing near Wedge Island off the southwestern coast of Australia. They had decided to cut short the fishing trip due to the rough seas. As they headed back to port, the engine sputtered and then cut out. The boat was now adrift. It was 11:30 AM and nobody expected them back until late afternoon.

The 59-ft. cabin cruiser was tossed about by 7 ft. high waves. About two miles from shore, the boat capsized and its occupants were thrown into the rough seas. The teens clung to the hull of the upturned boat. There were lifejackets on board, but nobody was wearing them. Trent tried to swim under the boat and retrieve the lifejackets, which were safely stowed underneath the bow of the boat, but the seas were too rough; he couldn't get into the storage area. Flares, which would have alerted those on shore to their situation, were also *safely* stowed under the bow.

to the Rescue

Trent Gardner (left) and **Ross Weaver** (right) show off their silver medals

With the boat slowly sinking and no lifejackets to keep them afloat, Ross made the decision to swim to shore to bring back help. Trent offered to go with him. They set off together. High waves, a strong current, forceful sea breezes, and shark-infested waters were major obstacles for Trent and Ross.

The wind and waves set them off course, and what should have been a two-mile swim turned into an five-to-six mile nightmare. But both teens made it to shore. Cold and exhausted, Trent even volunteered to return to the capsized boat with the rescuers. They found the four people who had stayed with the boat clinging to the small section of the bow that was left above the water.

Both Ross and Trent were awarded silver medals by the Royal Humane Society of Australasia Inc. The RHSA gives public recognition to acts of bravery by those who risk their own lives in saving or attempting to save the lives of others. The RHSA has made 7,414 awards since 1874.

CHECKPOINT
Notice all the challenges that faced Trent and Ross.

wrap up

1. What traits do you think Ross and Trent have that earned them their silver medal?

2. Write a newspaper report about Ross and Trent's experience.

SHARK ATTACK

By Jan TenBruggencate

Shark bites off left arm of teenage Kaua'i surfer

HONOLULU ADVERTISER, November 1, 2003

LIHU'E, Kaua'i — Hawaii's surfing community was in shock yesterday after a shark bit off the left arm of 13-year-old Bethany Hamilton, one of the state's top competitive surfers.

"One of our precious young people was attacked by a shark," said Kaua'i Fire Department Battalion Chief Bob Kaden, choking up at a news conference yesterday.

The young surfer, a rising star, had been surfing the West Reef area fronting Tunnels Beach in Ha'ena with her best friend, fellow competitor Alana Blanchard, 13, and Blanchard's father, Holt.

There had been considerable rain, but the water was clear, said Kaden, who has been teaching his own daughter to surf.

Surfers said a large shark had been seen in the area a few days earlier, but Kaden said no one saw the 7:30 AM attack. "There was no warning," he said.

A surfer reported hearing Bethany scream in pain or shock and then yell to warn others, Kaden said.

---

warm up

- Shark Attack! What images do you have from movies and TV shows about sharks?

- What do we know about Bethany Hamilton from her picture?

CHECKPOINT

How many of the five Ws, (who, what, when, where, and why) does the first paragraph of this news report answer?

FYI

The relative risk of a shark attack is very small. Many more people are killed worldwide by bees, elephants, or lightning.

> "She's going to become the world's champion. She's got drive. She's real sweet. I think her potential is still there."

C H E C K P O I N T →

Why did Bethany's mother, Cheri Hamilton, believe Holt Blanchard's quick action saved Bethany's life?

"She yelled, 'Shark! Shark!' At first the people around her thought she was kidding. Then they saw her trying to paddle herself to shore with one arm," he said.

She had lost her arm from just below the shoulder, according to a statement issued by her family. Her board had a gaping hole on its left side, 17 inches wide at the rail and extending to within an inch of the board's center stringer.

Fellow surfers quickly put her on another board and began paddling her the several hundred yards to shore. Family friend Holt Blanchard used a surf leash to apply a tourniquet to stop the bleeding.

"Bethany's mother, Cheri Hamilton, attributes Holt's quick action to saving her daughter's life," the family statement said.

Bethany was carried ashore on a surfboard and placed in a pickup truck to await the ambulance. "She remained conscious," Kaden said. "The tourniquet, direct pressure on the wound, and the effects of shock reduced the bleeding," he said. An ambulance crew started intravenous fluids as soon as it arrived.

Hanalei fireman Tim Terrazas holding Bethany's surfboard

Surf Board–AP Photo/The Garden Island, Dennis Fujimoto; Bethany Hamilton on surfboard–AP Photo/Ronen Zilberman

She was taken to Wilcox Hospital, where the family said "she is expected to recover."

Bobby Cocke, owner of the Kai Kane classic surf shop in Hanalei, who has known Bethany and her family all her life, said he fully expects Bethany to be back in competitive surfing.

"She's going to become the world's champion. She's got drive. She's real sweet. I think her potential is still there," he said.

Bethany, who is home-schooled, surfs on the team of Hanalei Surf Co. owner, Charlie Cowden. Cowden was at the hospital with the family yesterday. He said the attack is getting national attention. "Everybody's just shocked. Everybody in the whole surfing community is calling to support her," he said.

Cowden, like Cocke, said he expects her to do well. "It's heartbreaking to have someone 13 years old have this limitation on her, but she's a tough little girl. She's really a champion," he said.

Although no one reported seeing the shark, and the tooth imprints on the board have not yet been studied, most surfers and firefighters believe it was a tiger shark because of some classic characteristics: a single attack in the surf zone near dawn or dusk, with no follow-up.

Acting fire Capt. Steve Fountain at the Hanalei substation, which responded to the attack, said fishermen who saw Bethany's surfboard estimated the shark could have been 12 to 15 feet long.

Firefighters on jet-powered watercraft and a rescue boat unsuccessfully searched the waters at Tunnels for Bethany's arm in hopes it could be reattached.

CHECKPOINT

Why did people believe this setback would not stop Bethany from becoming a world champion surfer?

wrap up

Write a summary for an adult to inform him or her about what happened to Bethany Hamilton. "Chunk" the paragraphs in the article so that your summary contains no more than three paragraphs.

SUBWAY SAVIOR

MAN LEAPS TO SUBWAY TRACKS, SAVES LIFE
HUNDREDS STAND BY AND MERELY WATCH

By Dale Anne Freed

warm up

- In a classroom discussion, share your reactions to the headlines.

- How do you think you would have reacted if you had been there?

CHECKPOINT

Notice the evidence that shows that this rescue was a "close call."

September 17, 2003

Petru George Ciorau can't understand why hundreds of rush hour commuters did nothing to rescue a woman who lost her balance and fell on the tracks.

"Those people froze. That's what I found kind of strange," said Ciorau, 22, who didn't think twice about rescuing the slight Kaur-Hayer Harbajan, a 58-year-old woman in an apricot-colored sari who'd been waiting on the Yonge-Bloor platform with her husband for a Monday morning train.

"This kid is a bona fide hometown hero," said acting fire captain Jim Dillon, who was called to the scene. "He put his life on the line to save somebody he'd never met and probably will never meet again."

Harbajan, who doesn't speak English, was uninjured and "overwhelmed" by her rescue, said Dillon.

As he jumped on the tracks, Ciorau could see the train coming toward him.

"I didn't know what to do. I was thinking of asking for somebody to help me (lift Harbajan on to the platform). But they were frozen. So I switched to Plan B … I know that if you go to the wall, you're safe."

bona fide: *genuine*

So Ciorau lifted the woman up, crossed over the tracks, luckily missing contact with the 600-volt power rail, and carried Harbajan safely to the wall.

Veteran subway driver Dominic Guerrero, coming into the Yonge-Bloor station on a westbound train, saw the pair on the tracks and hit his emergency brake — stopping 1.5 metres (5 ft.) away.

"I don't really see it as something amazing. It's really just something I would do," said Ciorau who had just come off night duty at a supermarket, where he works stocking shelves. "I was wondering why most people wouldn't do that. If that's my mom down there and some people are watching I would want someone to jump in," he said.

FYI

The world's first subway opened in London, England, in 1863, with steam locomotives.

The first U.S. subway opened in October, 1904. The subway fare was 5¢ for the next 42 years.

CHECKPOINT

Why do few people stop to help?

CHECKPOINT

Notice the words and phrases used to show how different Petru Ciorau is from the crowd.

"It's classic that few stop to help," said Toronto psychiatrist Dr. Greg Dubord. "Everybody thinks somebody else will help," explained Dubord, director of the Toronto Centre for Cognitive Therapy.

The passive bystander phenomenon has been studied extensively since the 1964 New York City murder of Kitty Genovese. She was heard screaming by dozens of nearby residents, "none of whom offered assistance or even phoned for help until it was too late," Dubord said. "It's a fairly standard part of social psychology texts."

Dubord described Ciorau as a "little more in touch with his instincts and he's a little more of an independent thinker and he's got less of a herd mentality, which is good."

"He sees an opportunity to help. He doesn't look around to see if everybody with suits is helping. He just helps."

Now, Ciorau is thinking about joining the fire department.

"I'd like to talk to some firefighters and find out more about the job," he said.

While he may not want to be recognized, the Romanian-born man who came to Canada with his family in 1989 to make a better life, is going to receive an Award of Merit from the Toronto Transit Commission.

---

classic: *typical*
social psychology: *study of behavior of people in groups*
herd mentality: *mindless following of a group's behavior*

wrap up

1. Create a flow chart, highlighting the actions taken by Ciorau.

2. With a partner, brainstorm words and phrases, not in the article, to describe Ciorau and his actions.

3. In the role of a bystander who watched Ciorau's rescue of Harbajan, describe the events in a journal entry or an email to a friend.

EUGÉNE RUTAGARAMA
AKA MR. GORILLA

RWANDA

Tanzania

Burundi

Rwanda has always had a troubled history. There have been internal tribal fighting, and conflicts with European colonial powers and neighboring countries. Conflict between Tutsi and Hutu tribes in 1959 led to thousands being killed. Rwanda gained independence in 1962, and the majority Hutus took control of the government. In 1994, Rwanda suffered one of the most horrific events in history. Within only three months, over 800,000 people were killed, the vast majority of them Tutsis. The genocide by the ruling Hutu majority was sparked by the death of the Hutu president, Juvénal Habyarimana, who died in a plane crash on April 6, 1994.

genocide: *killing an entire group of people*

warm up

Do you think it is important to stop the extinction of animals? Why or why not?

C H E C K P O I N T

As you read the following paragraphs, notice the effects of the Rwandan conflict on Eugène Rutagarama and his family, the Rwandan population, and the mountain gorillas.

In times of conflict, doing what seems normal can be extraordinary. Eugène Rutagarama struggled to make sense of the ethnic conflict that divided his country. Between 1959 and 1994, ethnic wars forced Eugène and his family to flee Rwanda four times. Most of his relatives, including his parents and two brothers, died during the conflicts. Eugène had to live much of his teen years in exile in Burundi.

To help him survive the turmoil, he focused on saving gorillas, the gentle giants of the mountains. "The lesson is to have an ideal and stay committed to it. I was convinced conservation was my life. The trick is not to be sidetracked by politics and prejudices."

War threatened to destroy one of Rwanda's natural resources and a huge source of income — the mountain gorillas that live in Volcano National Park. Wealthy tourists pay up to $500 to spend an hour observing the animals in their natural habitat. Only tea and coffee exports bring more to Rwanda's economy. Eugène saw in the gorillas a way to help his country rebuild economically while saving the gorillas from extinction. "Most Rwandans don't know or understand why anyone would want to work with gorillas. I was concerned by the rate of disappearance of gorillas. I chose them because they are very different from all other animals; they are between people and animals!"

In 1991, Eugène was working for the Rwandan Office of Tourism and National Parks (ROTNP) when the Hutu government imprisoned him. He was studying the growth of bamboo, the main source of food in the gorillas' diet, to see what effect the growing human population was having on the gorillas' natural habitat. The Hutu government claimed that Eugène was aiding Tutsi rebels by creating a map for them to find their way through Volcano National Park.

While in prison, Eugène's spirits did not fail. He got the inmates to lead daily prayers and compete in card games. For himself, he educated the prisoners about the conservation of the mountain gorillas, earning himself the nickname "Mr. Gorilla."

Eugène was rescued in 1991 by the Rwandese Patriotic Front, and he fled to nearby Burundi. In 1994, Eugène abandoned the safety of Burundi to return to the conflict in Rwanda to direct the National Parks program. "There are a lot of people taking care of people. There aren't many who are concerned for the gorillas."

---

ethnic: *refers to a tribal or nationality group*
turmoil: *violent confusion*

Eugene Rutagarama–photo courtesy of Goldman Environmental Foundation; Gorilla–©Getty Images/PhotoDisc\44054

Despite the fact that he could have been killed transporting money and supplies to Volcano National Park in the Virunga Mountains, Eugène Rutagarama continued to carry out his duties as an employee of the Rwandan Office of Tourism and National Parks.

Traveling through the park was very dangerous. The possibility of ambush by the Hutu militia, who were known to select and kill certain people on the road, made it very risky. Eugène had to travel through the park to make the presence of the ROTNP known. For two years, park rangers patrolled the park along with Rwandese Patriotic Army patrols to make sure the goals of gorilla conservation were met. Eugène was able to meet park rangers who had not been paid for five years to make sure protected areas of the park were not destroyed by the resettlement of two million refugees returning after the war.

In 1994, Eugène began the task of convincing the new government that tourism would bring money to Rwanda and that the natural habitat of the mountain gorillas had to be saved. After the horror of genocide, a common goal to preserve something of shared value can help Rwandans rebuild their country. In 2001, the gorilla population had grown by 11 percent, thanks to the efforts of people like Eugène Rutagarama.

FYI

People pose the biggest threat to gorillas. Poaching carries a double risk: being killed by the mother gorilla or being arrested by the police.

The mountain gorillas are a national symbol. Each page of a Rwandan passport is watermarked with the image of a gorilla.

Mountain gorillas live up to 53 years in captivity, but there are no mountain gorillas in captivity today. About 650 mountain gorillas are alive in the wild today.

Scientific researchers, like the late Dian Fossey whose life was illustrated in the movie *Gorillas in the Mist*, study the gorillas in their natural habitat hoping to better understand the connection between humans and apes.

wrap up

1. Write a series of five subheadings to capture the main points throughout this article.

2. What are three things Eugene did to help stop the extinction of Rwanda's mountain gorillas?

3. Create a poster to raise money to help save the mountain gorillas of Rwanda.

WEB CONNECTIONS

Go to one of the following websites to find out more about what you can do to help the mountain gorillas. Use the information to write a letter to a business in your area asking for a donation to help save mountain gorillas.

www.dianfossey.org
www.cotf.edu/ete/modules/mgorilla/mgorilla.html
www.koko.org

Afghan Women's
Olympic
DREAM

June 2004

CHECKPOINT

Why do you think the author chose to use question marks for some of the answers?

Imagine that you are talented enough to compete in the Olympic Games but are prevented from doing so because your country has been suspended from the games. How would you feel? Angry, perhaps frustrated? How about relieved when your country is finally allowed to compete? That is exactly how Robina Muqimyar, a 100-meter sprinter, and Friba Rezihi, who will compete in judo, felt when told they could represent Afghanistan at the 2004 Olympic Games in Athens.

"Afghanistan was suspended from the Olympic Games in 1999 for its discrimination against women and the Taliban rulers prevented athletes from training and the national stadium was used to host beatings and executions. Under the Taliban, a woman could not walk down the street without having a man with her, let alone compete in the Olympic Games. Despite this, Robina has decided to use her pent-up anger from past injustices to give her an edge in competition. "I learned from the Taliban to be oppressed," she said. "I'm going to teach people how to struggle against them, how to learn, and how to get whatever you want in life."

In their quest to make their Olympic dreams come true, both Robina and Friba traveled to Greece to train there. Both women are extremely grateful to the Greek government for allowing them the opportunity to use the country's training facilities. In the stadium in Kabul, Afghanistan, runners have to train on a broken concrete track.

While it is highly unlikely that the women will win Olympic medals, Friba believes that "it's like a gold medal for us to participate as Afghan women after a long, long time." In fact, Robina and Friba will be the first women to represent Afghanistan at the Olympics.

While there are many cheering for these Olympic hopefuls, there are several who believe that Afghanistan's strict Islamic dress code should prevent the women from competing in the games. However, in order to comply with the Islamic dress code which requires women to cover everything except their hands, face, and feet, both Robina and Friba will wear full-length track suits that cover their legs. But, that doesn't bother Robina and Friba; they are happy to wear whatever they are told to wear so long as they can still compete.

Taliban: *political and religious militia that gained power in Afghanistan in the mid-1990s*
pent-up: *built up*
comply: *obey*

FYI

Robina Muqimyar and Friba Rezihi were, in 2004, the first Afghan women to compete in any Olympic event. They may not have been Olympic stars but they made history.

CHECKPOINT

Notice this quotation by Robina. What character trait is she showing?

wrap up

1. List the restrictions Robina and Friba had placed on them when the Taliban was in power.

2. What simile does Robina use to describe what participation in the Olympic games means for her and Friba?

3. Write a newspaper headline announcing the arrival of Robina and Friba at the Olympics.

BLIND TO FAILURE

ERIK WEIHENMAYER

CHECKPOINT
Notice the many ways one could die on Mount Everest. Why does the author mention these terrible things at this point in the article?

Mountaineers scoffed at the notion that Erik Weihenmayer, sightless since he was 13, could climb Everest. But a killer peak is no obstacle for a man who can conquer adversity.

When he saw Erik Weihenmayer arrive that afternoon, Pasquale Scaturro began to have misgivings about the expedition he was leading. Here they were on the first floor of Mount Everest, and Erik — the reason for the whole trip — was stumbling into Camp 1 bloody, sick, and dehydrated. ...

As Erik passed out in his tent, the rest of the team gathered in a worried huddle. "I was thinking maybe this is not a good idea," says Scaturro. ... "This blind guy barely makes it to Camp 1?"

This blind guy, Erik Weihenmayer, 33, wasn't just another yuppie trekker who'd lost a few rounds to the mountain. Blind since he was 13, the victim of a rare hereditary disease of the retina, he began attacking mountains in his early 20s.

But he had been having the same doubts as the rest of the team. ... There are so many ways to die on that mountain, spanning the spectacular (fall through an ice shelf into a crevasse, get waylaid by an avalanche, develop cerebral edema from lack of oxygen, and have your brain literally swell out of your skull) and the banal (become disoriented because of oxygen deprivation and decide you'll take a little nap, right here, in the snow, which becomes a forever nap).

adversity: *difficulty*
crevasse: *a deep crack, usually in a glacier*
banal: *ordinary*
deprivation: *shortage*

CHECKPOINT
Notice the simile that shows Erik's blindness could not be avoided. Why is this an effective comparison?

Erik, as he stumbled through the icefall, was so far out of his comfort zone that he began to speculate on which of those fates might await him. ...

The blind thrive on patterns: stairs are all the same height, city blocks roughly the same length, curbs approximately the same depth. They learn to identify the patterns in their environment much more than the sighted population does, and to rely on them to plot their way through the world.

But in the Khumbu Icefall, the trail through the Himalayan glacier is patternless, a diabolically cruel obstacle course for a blind person. ...

CHECKPOINT
What do you think the author wants the reader to know about Erik?

[However], Erik is gifted with strong lungs, a refined sense of balance, a disproportionately powerful upper body, rubbery legs, and flexible ankles. His conditioning is exemplary and his heart rate low. ... On Everest, mental toughness is perhaps the most important trait a climber can have. "Erik is mentally one of the strongest guys you will ever meet," says fellow climber Chris Morris. ...

diabolically: *in an evil manner*
exemplary: *outstandingly good*

For Erik, who knew almost as soon as he could speak that he would lose his vision in his early teens, excelling as an athlete was the result of accepting his disability rather than denying it. His blindness was a medical inevitability, like a court date with a hanging judge. ...

Climbing with Erik isn't that different from climbing with a sighted mountaineer. You wear a bell on your pack, and he follows the sound, scuttling along using his custom-made climbing poles to feel his way along the trail. His climbing partners shout out helpful descriptions: "Death fall two feet to your right!" "Emergency helicopter-evacuation pad to your left!" He is fast, often running up the back of less experienced climbers. His partners all have scars from being jabbed by Erik's climbing poles when they slowed down. ...

Erik had some advantages as they closed in on the peak. For one thing, all the climbers wore goggles and oxygen masks, restricting their vision so severely that they could not see their own feet — a condition Erik was used to. Also, the final push for the summit began in the early evening, so most of the climb was in pitch darkness; the only illumination was from miners' lamps.

When Erik and the team began the final ascent from Camp 4 — the camp he describes as Dante's Inferno with ice and wind — they had been on the mountain for two months, climbing up and down and then up from Base Camp to Camps 1, 2, and 3, getting used to the altitude and socking away enough equipment — especially oxygen canisters — to make a summit push. They had tried for the summit once but had turned back because of weather. ...

On May 24, with only seven days left in the climbing season, most of the N.F.B. (National Federation for the Blind) expedition members knew this was their last shot at the peak. ... They were terribly disappointed when the sky lit up with lightning, driving snow, and fierce winds. "We thought we were done," Erik says. "We would have been spanked if we made a push in those conditions." A few teammates gambled and went for it, and Jeff Evans and Brad Bull heroically pulled out fixed guidelines that had been frozen in the ice. By the time Base Camp radioed that the storm was passing, Erik and the entire team were coated in 5 cm (2 in.) of snow. Inspired by the possibility of a break in the weather, the team pushed on. ... At that point the climbers looked like astronauts walking on some kind of Arctic moon. They moved slowly because of fatigue from their huge, puffy down suits, backpacks with oxygen canisters and regulators and goggles. ...

The weather was finally clearing as they reached the Hillary Step, the 12-meters (39.4 ft.) rock face that is the last major obstacle before the summit. Erik clambered up the cliff, bellyflopping over the top. "I celebrated with the dry heaves," he jokes. And then it was 45 minutes of walking up a sharply angled snow slope to the summit.

"Look around, dude," Evans told the blind man when they were standing on top of the world. "Just take a second and look around."

Dante's Inferno: *hell*

... [Erik] says summiting Everest was great, probably the greatest experience of his life. But then he thinks about a moment a few months ago, before Everest, when he was walking down the street in Colorado with daughter Emma in a front pack. They were on their way to buy some banana bread for his wife, and Emma was pulling on his hand, her little fingers curled around his index finger. That was a summit too, he says. There are summits everywhere. You just have to know where to look.

wrap up

1. Create a chart of Erik's climb of Mount Everest. Use the following headings: Difficulties any climber would face; Special difficulties Erik faced because he was blind; Advantages Erik had over the other climbers because he was blind.

2. Explain the irony of Evans' comment to Erik once they reached the top of Everest: "Look around, dude. Just take a second and look around." Do you think Evans meant to be nasty? Why or why not?

ACKNOWLEDGMENTS

The publisher gratefully acknowledges the following for permission to reprint copyrighted material in this book.

Every reasonable effort has been made to trace the owners of copyrighted material and to make due acknowledgment. Any errors or omissions drawn to our attention will be gladly rectified in future editions.

Andrea Damewood: "Teen Publisher Shares Her Story." Reprinted with permission.

John Davidson: "Jesse's Journey."

Dale Anne Freed: "Man leaps to subway tracks, saves life", *Toronto Star* (17 September 2003), reprinted with permission — Torstar Syndication Services.

Karl Taro Greenfeld: "Blind to Failure," *TIME Magazine,* Canadian edition (18 June 2001, Vol. 157, No. 24) and "Meet the Napster," *TIME Magazine* (2 October 2000, Vol. 156. No. 14). © 2004 TIME Inc. reprinted by permission (excerpt).

Richard Hill: *Skywalkers: a History of Indian Ironworkers*, Woodland Indian Cultural Educational Centre, 1987 (excerpt).

Brant Maracle: "The Call of the Reserve," *Skywalkers: a History of Indian Ironworkers*, Woodland Indian Cultural Educational Centre, 1987.

Jan TenBruggencate: "Shark Attack!" *The Honolulu Advertiser* (1 November 2003). Reprinted with permission.

"Victim's Champion is Killed in Iraq" by Ellen Knickmeyer from the *Washington Post*, Monday, April 18, 2005, pg. A13.